Zakynthos Travel Guide 2023

The Ultimate Guide to Explore the Unspoiled Natural Island of Zakynthos, Offering Insider Tips, Itineraries, and Recommendations For a Perfect Trip

Christopher L. Gerlach

Table of Contents

My First time In Zakynthos

It was a warm summer's day, and as I set foot on the shores of Zakynthos, a sense of anticipation filled the air. Little did I know that this unspoiled paradise would etch memories in my heart forever. As I strolled along the coastline, the azure waves caressed the golden sand, creating a symphony of tranquility. The sun's gentle rays kissed my skin, and a cool sea breeze whispered tales of ancient legends.

I found myself on Shipwreck Beach, standing in awe of nature's masterpiece. The towering cliffs stood sentinel, guarding the secrets of a bygone era. As I gazed at the rusted vessel resting gracefully on the shore, I couldn't help but ponder the stories it held within its timeworn walls. It was as if the echoes of the past whispered through the wind, captivating my soul.

But it wasn't just the breathtaking landscapes that moved me. It was the warmth and kindness of the locals that truly touched my heart. Their genuine smiles and welcoming gestures made me feel like a cherished friend, embracing me in their vibrant culture.

Zakynthos is not just an island; it's a tapestry of emotions woven with threads of beauty, history, and human connection. It's a place where time slows down, allowing you to immerse yourself in the moment and forge lasting memories.

Embark on your own journey to Zakynthos, and let it weave its magic around you.

1. Introduction

Welcome to the enchanting island of Zakynthos, a hidden gem nestled in the embrace of the Ionian Sea. This is a place where nature's wonders unfold at every turn, captivating the senses and leaving an indelible mark on the soul. Whether you're a seasoned traveler seeking new adventures or a curious explorer yearning to uncover unspoiled beauty this guide is for you.

In these pages, we invite you on a journey of discovery, where turquoise waters meet pristine sandy beaches, and lush landscapes stretch as far as the eye can see. Immerse yourself in the vibrant culture, explore hidden coves and ancient ruins, and indulge in the mouthwatering flavors of authentic Zakynthian cuisine. With insider tips, detailed itineraries, and invaluable recommendations, we ensure that every moment of your trip is filled with awe-inspiring experiences.

So, pack your sense of adventure and let the allure of Zakynthos beckon you. Whether you're a nature enthusiast, a history buff, or a sun-soaked wanderer, this guide will accompany you every step of the way, unveiling the island's secrets and ensuring that your journey is nothing short of perfection. Get ready to embark on the ultimate Zakynthos experience.

1.1 About Zakynthos

Nestled in the heart of the Ionian Sea, Zakynthos, also known as Zante, is a captivating Greek island that boasts a unique blend of natural beauty, rich history, and warm hospitality. With its pristine beaches, crystal-clear waters, and lush landscapes,

Zakynthos is a true paradise for nature enthusiasts and wanderers alike.

The island is renowned for its striking coastal cliffs, hidden coves, and secluded caves that beckon adventurers to explore their depths. From the iconic Shipwreck Beach, with its rusted vessel set against a backdrop of towering cliffs, to the mesmerizing Blue Caves, where sunlight dances on the azure waters, Zakynthos never fails to leave visitors awe-struck.

But Zakynthos is not just about its natural wonders. The island also has a vibrant cultural heritage waiting to be discovered. Zakynthos Town, the charming capital, offers a glimpse into the island's history with its Venetian architecture, picturesque squares, and fascinating museums.

1.2 Why Visit Zakynthos

Why should you choose Zakynthos as your next travel destination? The reasons are abundant. Zakynthos offers a perfect blend of adventure, relaxation, and cultural immersion, catering to a wide range of interests and desires.

For beach lovers, Zakynthos presents a plethora of stunning options. Whether you seek the iconic Shipwreck Beach, the secluded beauty of Porto Limnionas, or the nesting grounds of the endangered loggerhead sea turtles at Gerakas Beach, the island's coastline is an idyllic haven for sun-seekers and water enthusiasts.

Nature enthusiasts will be captivated by the island's biodiversity, as Zakynthos is home to rare flora and fauna. The Zakynthos National Marine Park, established to protect the endangered caretta-caretta sea turtles, offers a unique opportunity to witness these magnificent creatures in their natural habitat. Additionally, hiking trails across the island provide a chance to immerse oneself in the island's natural splendor.

History buffs will find Zakynthos a treasure trove of historical sites and landmarks. Explore the ancient ruins of Olympia, birthplace of the Olympic Games, or venture to the Venetian Castle in Zakynthos Town for a glimpse into the island's past.

Beyond its natural and historical allure, Zakynthos welcomes visitors with warm hospitality and a genuine embrace of its cultural traditions. Indulge in traditional Zakynthian cuisine, dance to the rhythm of traditional music at local festivals, and connect with the friendly locals who will make you feel like a part of their extended family.

Zakynthos is a destination that promises to awaken your senses, ignite your curiosity, and leave an imprint on your soul. It invites you to step off the beaten path and create memories that will last a lifetime. Get ready to explore the unspoiled natural beauty of Zakynthos and immerse yourself in its captivating spirit.

Packing List

When preparing for your trip to Zakynthos, it's essential to pack the right items to ensure a comfortable and enjoyable experience. Here's a complete packing list to help you get ready:

1. Clothing:
- Lightweight, breathable tops and t-shirts
- Shorts and skirts for hot days
- Comfortable walking shoes or sandals
- Swimwear for beach days
- A light sweater or jacket for chilly evenings
- Sunglasses and a hat for protection
- Beach cover-up or sarong
- Casual evening attire for dining out

2. Essentials:
- Passport and travel documents
- Travel insurance information

- Local currency (Euros) and credit/debit cards

- Travel adapter for electrical outlets

- Mobile phone and charger

- Camera or smartphone for capturing memories

- Medications and prescriptions, if needed

- A first aid kit with all the necessary supplies, including bandages, painkillers, and any prescription drugs.

3. Beach Essentials:

- Beach towel or mat

- Sunscreen with high SPF

- Beach umbrella or sunshade

- Waterproof phone case or pouch

- Snorkeling gear, if desired

- Beach toys and games for added fun

4. Miscellaneous:

- Reusable water bottle to stay hydrated

- Insect repellent to ward off mosquitoes

- Toiletries in travel-size (body wash, shampoo, conditioner, etc.)

- Travel towel for convenience

- Portable charger for your electronic devices

- Travel-sized laundry detergent for washing clothes

- Day backpack for excursions and beach trips

- Travel guidebook or map of Zakynthos

Keep in mind to pack for the season and climate you may experience while there. Checking the weather forecast before your trip is usually a good idea to make sure you're ready for any changes in the weather.

With this complete packing list, you'll have all the essentials to make the most of your adventure on the beautiful island of Zakynthos.

25 Best Things To do In Zakynthos

1. Visit Shipwreck Beach (Navagio): Marvel at the iconic shipwreck resting on a stunning sandy beach surrounded by towering cliffs.

2. Explore the Blue Caves: Take a boat tour and venture into the enchanting blue-hued caves, where sunlight creates a magical underwater world.

3. Discover Zakynthos Town: Wander through the charming streets, visit Solomos Square, explore the Venetian Castle, and immerse yourself in the island's rich history and culture.

4. Swim with Caretta-Caretta Turtles: Head to Laganas Bay or Marathonisi Island for a chance

to swim alongside these majestic endangered sea turtles.

5. Enjoy the View from Bohali Hill: Climb up to Bohali Hill for panoramic views of Zakynthos Town and the sparkling Ionian Sea.

6. Relax at Porto Limnionas: Unwind in this picturesque, secluded cove with crystal-clear turquoise waters perfect for swimming and snorkeling.

7. Take a Boat Trip to Marathonisi (Turtle Island): Visit the nesting site of the endangered sea turtles, explore the caves, and soak up the island's natural beauty.

8. Hike to Keri Cliffs: Embark on a scenic hike to the breathtaking Keri Cliffs and witness the stunning views of the rugged coastline.

9. Discover the Neda Waterfalls: Venture inland to the neighboring Peloponnese region and immerse yourself in the beauty of the Neda Waterfalls, surrounded by lush greenery.

10. Enjoy Watersports: Try your hand at various watersports such as jet skiing, kayaking, paddleboarding, and parasailing at the island's beaches.

11. Explore the Traditional Village of Volimes: Experience the authentic Zakynthian village life, taste local delicacies, and shop for handmade crafts and souvenirs.

12. Visit the Monastery of Agios Dionysios: Pay homage to the patron saint of Zakynthos and explore the beautiful monastery dedicated to Agios Dionysios.

13. Dive into the Clear Waters of Xigia Beach: Take a refreshing swim in the rejuvenating sulphur-rich waters of Xigia Beach, known for their therapeutic properties.

14. Go Wine Tasting: Discover the island's winemaking traditions by visiting local vineyards and tasting Zakynthian wines, such as Verdea and Avgoustiatis.

15. Enjoy Sunset Views at Cameo Island: Savor the magical ambiance as the sun sets over the sea while relaxing at the picturesque Cameo Island.

16. Explore the Venetian Castle of Zakynthos Town: Climb to the top of the Venetian Castle ruins for panoramic views and a glimpse into the island's history.

17. Indulge in Zakynthian Cuisine: Sample traditional dishes like moussaka, pastitsio, and local specialties like rabbit stifado and stuffed tomatoes.

18. Relax on Gerakas Beach: Unwind on this pristine, sandy beach nestled in the Zakynthos National Marine Park and admire the nesting grounds of the sea turtles.

19. Attend Local Festivals and Events: Immerse yourself in Zakynthian culture by participating in vibrant festivals like the Carnival, celebrating Easter traditions, or enjoying live music performances.

20. Discover the Venetian Village of Kampi: Wander through the picturesque village of Kampi, known for its Venetian architecture, stunning views, and delicious local cuisine.

21. Go Snorkeling or Scuba Diving: Explore the vibrant underwater world of Zakynthos, filled with colorful marine life, by snorkeling or scuba diving at various diving spots around the island.

22. Experience Traditional Zakynthian Music: Attend a live performance of traditional Zakynthian music and dance, known as Kalamatianos, to immerse yourself in the island's cultural heritage.

23. Take a Jeep Safari: Embark on an off-road adventure through Zakynthos' rugged terrain, discovering hidden gems, olive groves, and charming villages along the way.

24. Visit the Venetian Fortress of Zakynthos Town: Explore the imposing Venetian Fortress, also known as Castle of Zakynthos, and enjoy panoramic views of the town and surrounding landscapes.

25. Enjoy a Sunset Boat Cruise: Set sail on a sunset boat cruise around the island, watching the sky ablaze with colors as the sun dips below the horizon, creating a truly magical experience.

2. Planning Your Trip

2.1 Best Time to Visit Zakynthos

The Perfect Season

Summer and spring are the two best times to visit Zakynthos. Due to the pleasant and sunny weather, summer is the most popular season for travel. Although the island can be very crowded in the summer, spring is a terrific time to visit if you're seeking for a more laid-back getaway.

Summer

Summer is the peak season in Zakynthos, and the weather is warm and sunny from June to September. The average temperature in July and August is around 85 degrees Fahrenheit, and the water temperature is perfect for swimming.

This is the best time to visit if you want to enjoy all that Zakynthos has to offer, including its beaches, water sports, and nightlife.

Spring

If you want a holiday that is a little more laid back, spring is a fantastic season to go to Zakynthos. Even though it's still nice and sunny outside, fewer people are present. Around 75 degrees Fahrenheit is the usual temperature in May and June, and the water is still warm enough for swimming. If you want to take in the island's natural beauty and explore its historical attractions, now is a fantastic time to go.

Other Considerations

In addition to the weather, there are a few other factors to consider when choosing when to visit Zakynthos. For example, if you're interested in seeing the sea turtles that nest on Zakynthos' beaches, you'll want to visit between May and September. And if you're planning on doing any hiking, you'll want to avoid the hottest months of July and August.

No matter what time of year you choose to visit Zakynthos, you're sure to have a wonderful time. Just be sure to plan ahead so that you can enjoy all that the island has to offer.

Additional Information

The best time to see the sea turtles is between May and September.

The best time to go hiking is in the spring or fall.

The weather in Zakynthos is generally mild, but it can get hot in the summer.

The island is busiest in the summer, so if you're looking for a more relaxed vacation, spring is a good option.

2.2 Travel Insurance

Before you book your flights and accommodations, there's one important thing you need to do: get travel insurance.

Travel insurance is a policy that covers you in case of unexpected events during your trip, such as medical emergencies, flight cancellations, or lost luggage. It's like a safety net that can help you if things go wrong.

I know, I know. Travel insurance can be expensive. But it's worth it for the peace of mind it gives you. Imagine being on your dream vacation and then getting sick or injured.

Without travel insurance, you could be stuck with thousands of dollars in medical bills.

Or, what if your flight gets cancelled? Without travel insurance, you might have to pay for a new flight out of your own pocket. And if your luggage gets lost, you could be without your clothes, toiletries, and other essentials for the rest of your trip.

You can use travel insurance to pay for all of these expenses and more. Therefore, don't forget to purchase travel insurance whether you're planning a vacation to Zakynthos or anywhere else in the world. It's one of the finest strategies to guard against unforeseen costs.

The following are some advantages of purchasing travel insurance:

Medical coverage: If you get sick or injured while you're traveling, travel insurance can help you cover the cost of medical treatment. This can be especially important if you're traveling to a country with a different healthcare system than your own.

Trip cancellation and interruption coverage: If your trip is cancelled or interrupted due to unforeseen circumstances, travel insurance can help you get a refund for your non-refundable travel expenses. This could include things like flights, hotels, and tours.

Baggage loss and damage coverage: If your luggage is lost or damaged while you're traveling, travel insurance can help you cover the cost of replacing your belongings.

Emergency medical transportation coverage: If you need to be medically evacuated from your destination, travel insurance can help you cover the cost of the transportation.

Here are some recommendations for selecting travel insurance:

Examine many policies to locate one that suits your requirements and price range. Verify the policy's coverage for the exact activities you'll be engaging in while on vacation.

Carefully read the fine print to see what is and isn't covered. As soon as you make your travel arrangements, buy travel insurance.

2.3 Visa and Travel Documents

Before you can start packing your bags, there are a few things you need to do to make sure you have all the necessary visa and travel documents.

Visas

Most visitors to Zakynthos do not need a visa to enter Greece. However, citizens of some countries do need to obtain a visa in advance. You can check the requirements for your country on the website of the Greek Ministry of Foreign Affairs.

If a visa is required, you can apply for one at a Greek embassy or consulate abroad. Start early because the application process can take many weeks.

Travel Documents

In addition to your passport, you will also need to have a valid visa (if required), a return ticket, and proof of accommodation. You may also be asked to show evidence of sufficient funds to support your stay in Greece.

Your passport must be valid for at least six months after your planned departure date from Greece. You should also make sure that your passport has at least two blank pages for stamps.

Your return ticket should be for a flight or ferry that leaves Greece after your planned stay.

Your proof of accommodation can be a hotel reservation, a rental car agreement, or a letter from a friend or family member who lives in Greece.

Evidence of Sufficient Funds

The Greek authorities may ask you to show evidence that you have sufficient funds to support your stay in Greece. This could include a bank statement, a credit card statement, or a letter from your employer stating your salary.

The Bottom Line

Getting the necessary visa and travel documents can be a bit of a hassle, but it's worth it to make sure you're able to enjoy your trip to Zakynthos without any problems. So, start planning early and get all your paperwork in order.

Here are some additional tips for getting your visa and travel documents:

Check the requirements for your country as early as possible.

Make sure you have all the required documentation and begin the application process as soon as feasible.

Be prepared to discuss your trip intentions with others.

 Be patient and persistent.

2.4 Traveling to Zakynthos

2.4.1 By Air

Zakynthos is easily accessible by air, with direct flights from many major European cities. The island's airport (ZTH) is located just a few kilometers from Zakynthos Town, the capital. Flights from Athens are also available, and take about an hour.

Here are some of the benefits of traveling to Zakynthos by air:

 It's the fastest and most convenient way to get to the island.

There are direct flights from many major cities, so you can easily find a flight that fits your schedule.

The airport is located close to Zakynthos Town, so you can easily get to your hotel or other destination.

Here are some of the drawbacks of traveling to Zakynthos by air:

It can be more expensive than traveling by sea.

There may be delays or cancellations due to bad weather.

2.4.2 By Sea

Zakynthos can also be reached by ferry from several ports in Greece, including Athens, Kythira, and Kefalonia. The ferry journey takes about 4-5 hours from Athens, and 2-3 hours from Kythira and Kefalonia.

Here are some of the benefits of traveling to Zakynthos by sea:

It's a more scenic way to travel to the island.

It's often less expensive than traveling by air.

You can bring your own car or motorbike on the ferry, which gives you more flexibility when you're on the island.

Here are some of the drawbacks of traveling to Zakynthos by sea:

It's a slower way to travel to the island.

There may be delays or cancellations due to bad weather.

The best choice

The best way to travel to Zakynthos depends on your individual preferences and budget. If you're looking for the fastest and most convenient way to get to the island, then flying is the best option. If you're on a budget or want to enjoy a more scenic journey, then traveling by sea is a good choice.

No matter which way you choose, you're sure to have a great time on Zakynthos!

Here are some additional tips for traveling to Zakynthos:

 Book your flights or ferry tickets in advance, especially if you're traveling during the peak season.

Check the weather forecast before you travel, and be prepared for delays or cancellations due to bad weather.

If you're traveling by sea, bring some snacks and drinks with you, as the journey can be long.

Allow plenty of time to get to the airport or ferry port, especially if you're traveling during the peak season.

Enjoy your trip!

2.5 Getting Around Zakynthos

2.5.1 Public Transportation

Zakynthos is a relatively small island, so it's easy to get around by public transportation. The bus system is the most efficient way to get around, and there are also a few taxi companies and car rental agencies on the island.

Buses

The bus system in Zakynthos is run by KTEL Zakynthos, and there are buses that run to most of the major towns and villages on the island. The buses are relatively inexpensive, and they're a great way to see the island and meet some locals.

Taxis

There are a few taxi companies on Zakynthos, and they're a convenient way to get around if you're in a hurry or if you're traveling with a group. Taxis are relatively expensive, but they're not as expensive as they are in some other European cities.

Car Rental

If you want to have more flexibility and freedom to explore the island, you can rent a car. There are a few car rental agencies on Zakynthos, and they offer a variety of cars to choose from. Car rental is relatively expensive, but it can be a great way to see the island at your own pace.

Which Transportation Option Is Right for You?

Your budget, travel preferences, and schedule will all affect which mode of transportation is most appropriate for you. The bus is your best choice if money is short. You can rent a car if you'd like additional flexibility. Additionally, if you're traveling in a group, taxis can be a practical choice.

Here are some tips for getting around Zakynthos by public transportation:

Buy a bus pass if you're planning on doing a lot of traveling.

Be aware of the schedules, as they can vary depending on the time of year.

Ask the locals for help if you're not sure how to get somewhere.

2.5.2 Rental Cars and Scooters

Rental Cars

Renting a car is a great way to get around Zakynthos, especially if you want to explore the island at your own pace. There are many different car rental companies on the island, so you can be sure to find one that fits your budget and needs.

Pros of Renting a Car

Ability to travel to locations not reachable by public transit

More room for luggage and other things

Freedom to explore the island at your own speed

Cons of Renting a Car

Can be expensive, especially if you rent for a long period of time

Can be difficult to drive in the narrow streets of Zakynthos Town

Parking can be difficult, especially in popular areas

Rental Scooters

Renting a scooter is another great way to get around Zakynthos. Scooters are more affordable than cars, and they're a lot of fun to drive. However, they're also more dangerous, so it's important to be careful if you choose to rent a scooter.

Pros of Renting a Scooter

Affordable

Fun to drive

Easy to park

Can get you to places that are not accessible by car

Cons of Renting a Scooter

Can be dangerous, especially if you're not a experienced driver

Not as comfortable as a car

Can be difficult to drive in the narrow streets of Zakynthos Town

So, a rental scooter or a rental car is better for you? Your wants and choices actually matter. A rental car is the best option if you want the flexibility to explore the island at your own leisure and don't mind spending a bit more money. A rental scooter is a terrific choice if you're on a tight budget and seeking a more entertaining and adventurous mode of transportation.

Tips for Renting a Scooter or Car

Conduct research and contrast renting rates from various businesses.
Ensure that your driver's license is up to date.
Get coverage.

46

Recognize the regional traffic regulations.

Always drive defensively.

Renting a car or scooter is a great way to get around Zakynthos. With a little planning, you can find the perfect option for your needs and budget. So what are you waiting for? Start planning your trip today!

2.5.3 Taxis and Private Transfers

Taxis are a convenient way to get around Zakynthos, but they can be expensive. If you're traveling with a group, a private transfer may be a better option.

Taxis

Taxis are readily available in Zakynthos Town and at the airport. They are metered, but the rates can be high, especially if you're traveling from one side of the island to the other.

Private Transfers

Private transfers are a great way to get around Zakynthos if you're traveling with a group or if you want to avoid the hassle of taxis. You can book a private transfer through your hotel or a travel agency.

Which is Right for You?

So, between private transports and taxis, which is best for you? Your needs and financial situation actually determine this. Taxis could be the solution if money is tight. A private transfer, however, can be a better choice if you're traveling in a group or if you prefer the comfort of a private vehicle.

Here are some things to keep in mind when choosing between taxis and private transfers:

Cost: Taxis are generally less expensive than private transfers, but the difference can be significant if you're traveling with a group.

Convenience: Private transfers are more convenient than taxis, as you won't have to worry about hailing a cab or finding one that's available.

Flexibility: Private transfers are more flexible than taxis, as you can be picked up and dropped off at any location.

Here are some tips for getting the best deal on taxis and private transfers:

Book in advance: If you can, book your taxis or private transfers in advance. This will ensure that you have a car waiting for you when you arrive and that you won't have to pay any hidden fees.

Negotiate: If you're taking a taxi, don't be afraid to negotiate the fare. You may be able to get a lower price, especially if you're traveling during the off-season.

Compare prices: There are a number of websites that allow you to compare prices for taxis and private transfers. Finding the best offer will be aided by this.

No matter which option you choose, getting around Zakynthos is easy and convenient. So relax, enjoy the ride, and let someone else do the driving!

2.6 Accommodation Options

Zakynthos is a popular tourist destination, so there are many different accommodation options available to suit all budgets. Here is a brief overview of the different types of hotels and resorts you can find on the island:

Luxury Hotels: If you're looking for a truly luxurious stay, Zakynthos has a number of five-star hotels to choose from. These hotels offer all the amenities you could imagine, including private beaches, infinity pools, and world-class spas.

[Example: Romanos Beach Hotel & Suites]

Boutique Hotels: For a more intimate and stylish stay, consider booking a room at one of Zakynthos's boutique hotels. These hotels are often located in charming old town settings and offer a more personalized experience.

[Example: Gerakas Bay Boutique Hotel]

Family-Friendly Hotels: Zakynthos is a great place to visit with kids, and there are a number of family-friendly hotels on the island. These hotels typically have pools, kids' clubs, and other amenities that are perfect for families.

[Example: Tsilivi Beach Hotel]

Budget Hotels: If you're on a tight budget, there are still plenty of great accommodation options available on Zakynthos. There are a number of budget hotels located in the popular tourist areas, and these hotels offer basic but comfortable accommodations.

[Example: Ketty's Rooms]

2.6.1 Hotels and Resorts

Hotels and resorts are the most popular type of accommodation on Zakynthos. They offer a wide range of amenities, from private beaches to infinity pools. Here are a few of the best hotels and resorts on the island:

Amara Grand Resort: This five-star resort is located on a beautiful stretch of beach in Tsilivi. It offers stunning views of the Ionian Sea, as well as a number of luxury amenities, including a private beach, infinity pool, and spa.

Porto Zante Hotel & Resort: This four-star resort is located in the heart of Laganas. It's a great choice for families, as it has a number of kid-friendly amenities, including a kids' club and a playground.

Elysium Beach Hotel: This five-star resort is located on a secluded beach in Kalamaki. It's a great choice for couples, as it offers a romantic atmosphere and a number of couples-only amenities, including a private beach and a couples' spa.

The best way to choose the right hotel or resort for you is to consider your budget, your needs, and your interests. If you're looking for a luxurious stay with all the amenities, then one of the five-star hotels is a good option. If you're on a budget, then one of the budget hotels is a good option. And if you're traveling with kids, then one of the family-friendly hotels is a good option.

No matter what your budget or needs are, you're sure to find the perfect hotel or resort on Zakynthos.

2.6.2 Villas and Vacation Rentals

Villas and vacation rentals are a great option for those who want a more spacious and private accommodation option in Zakynthos. They offer a variety of amenities and features, such as swimming pools, private gardens, and multiple bedrooms. This makes them perfect for families, groups of friends, or couples who want to relax and enjoy their vacation in style.

What to look for in a villa or vacation rental

When choosing a villa or vacation rental in Zakynthos, there are a few things you should keep in mind:

 Location: Where do you want to be located? Do you want to be close to the beach, the town center, or a specific attraction?

 Size: How many people are in your group? What number of bedrooms and bathrooms are required?

 Features: Which amenities matter to you? Do you want a swimming pool, a private garden, or a washer and dryer?

Price: How much are you willing to spend?

Where to find villas and vacation rentals

There are a number of websites and agencies that can help you find villas and vacation rentals in Zakynthos. Some popular options include:

Booking.com
Airbnb
VRBO
HomeAway
TripAdvisor

Tips for booking a villa or vacation rental

Start your search early: The best villas and vacation rentals book up quickly, so it's important to start your search early.

Be flexible with your dates: If you're flexible with your dates, you'll have a better chance of finding a great deal.

Read the reviews: Before you book, be sure to read the reviews of the villa or vacation rental you're interested in. This will give you a good idea of what to expect.

Negotiate the price: If you're booking directly with the owner, don't be afraid to negotiate the price.

The best way to enjoy Zakynthos in elegance is to stay in a villa or vacation rental. With so many alternatives, you're sure to discover the ideal location to unwind and relish your holiday.

Here are some additional tips for finding and booking a villa or vacation rental in Zakynthos:

Consider the time of year: If you're planning on visiting during the peak season (June-August), be sure to book your villa or vacation rental well in advance.

Ask about discounts: Many villas and vacation rentals offer discounts for longer stays or for booking during the off-season.

Be aware of the cancellation policy: Before you book, be sure to read the cancellation policy carefully. This will help you avoid any surprises if you need to change your plans.

2.6.3 Camping and Glamping

Camping is a great way to experience the great outdoors and get back to nature. And, with its beautiful beaches and lush vegetation, Zakynthos is a perfect place to camp.

There are a few different camping options on Zakynthos, from basic campsites to more luxurious glamping resorts. If you're looking for a budget-friendly option, there are a few basic campsites located near the beaches. These campsites typically have basic facilities, such as shared bathrooms and showers, and they may or may not have electricity.

If you're looking for a more luxurious camping experience, there are a number of glamping resorts on Zakynthos. These resorts offer a variety of amenities, such as private tents, air conditioning, and even hot tubs.

No matter what your budget or preferences, there's a camping option on Zakynthos that's perfect for you.

Here are some of the benefits of camping and glamping in Zakynthos:

Get back to nature and experience the beauty of the island.
Take pleasure in the quietness of nature.

Make new friends from around the world.

Save money on accommodation.

Have a unique and memorable travel experience.

Here are some of the things to keep in mind when camping or glamping in Zakynthos:

The weather can be hot and humid in the summer, so be sure to pack accordingly.

There are a few different camping areas on the island, so be sure to do your research and choose one that's right for you.

If you're camping in a basic campsite, be prepared to share facilities with other campers.

If you're glamping, be sure to book your accommodation in advance, as these resorts are popular.

Here are some of the best camping and glamping spots on Zakynthos:

Camping Skopos: This campsite is located in the north of the island, near the village of Skopos. It has a variety of facilities, including shared bathrooms, showers, a laundry room, and a restaurant.

Glamping Village Zakynthos: This glamping resort is located in the south of the island, near the village of Kalamaki. It offers a variety of accommodation options, including private tents, air-conditioned tents, and even treehouses.

Camping Agios Ioannis: This campsite is located on the east coast of the island, near the village of Agios Ioannis. It has a beautiful beachfront location and offers a variety of facilities, including shared bathrooms, showers, a laundry room, and a restaurant.

3. Exploring Zakynthos

3.1 Zakynthos Town (Zante Town)

Zakynthos Town, also known as Zante Town, is the capital of Zakynthos island in Greece. It is a beautiful city with a rich history and culture. The town was founded by the Venetians in the 13th century, and it has been ruled by a number of different powers over the centuries, including the Turks, the French, and the British.

The town's old town is a UNESCO World Heritage Site, and it is home to a number of historical and cultural attractions, including the Venetian Castle, the Church of Saint Dionysius, and the Byzantine Museum. The town also has a number of lively bars and clubs, making it a popular destination for tourists.

3.1.2 Top Attractions

Venetian Castle: The Venetian Castle is one of the most iconic landmarks in Zakynthos Town. It was built in the 15th century by the Venetians, and it offers stunning views of the town and the surrounding area.

Church of Saint Dionysius: The Church of Saint Dionysius is the patron saint of Zakynthos. Built in the 17th century, it is a stunning church.

Byzantine Museum Byzantine artwork and artifacts can be found in the Byzantine Museum. It is an interesting museum that provides a window into Zakynthos' past.

Laganas Beach (Laganas) One of Zakynthos' most well-liked beaches is Laganas Beach. Long and sandy, it's the ideal beach for swimming, tanning, and water sports.

Navagio Beach: Navagio Beach is one of the most famous beaches in Zakynthos. It is a secluded beach that is only accessible by boat. The beach is known for its stunning white cliffs and its shipwreck, which is a popular tourist attraction.

Blue Caves: The Blue Caves are a series of sea caves that are located off the coast of Zakynthos. The caves are known for their beautiful blue waters, which are caused by the sunlight reflecting off the limestone rocks.

3.1.3 Local Cuisine and Dining

Zakynthos Town has a vibrant culinary scene, and there are a wide variety of restaurants to choose from. The town is home to traditional Greek restaurants, as well as restaurants serving international cuisine.

Some of the most popular dishes in Zakynthos Town include:

Souvlaki: Souvlaki is a grilled skewer of meat, typically pork or chicken. It is a popular street food in Greece, and it is often served with pita bread, tomatoes, onions, and tzatziki.

Moussaka: Moussaka is a traditional Greek dish made with eggplant, ground meat, potatoes, and a béchamel sauce. The recipe is tasty and filling, ideal for a chilly winter day.

Yoghurt with honey: Yoghurt with honey is a popular Greek dessert. It is made with thick Greek yoghurt and a drizzle of honey. It is a simple but delicious dessert that is perfect for a hot summer day.

There are also a number of bars and cafes in Zakynthos Town, making it a great place to enjoy a drink and people-watch.

3.2 Beaches and Coastal Areas

Zakynthos is home to some of the most beautiful beaches in the world, from the iconic Shipwreck Beach to the secluded Porto Limnionas. Here are four of the island's best beaches, along with tips on how to get to them:

3.2.1 Shipwreck Beach (Navagio)

Navagio Beach, also known as Shipwreck Cove, is one of the most popular tourist destinations in Zakynthos. The beach is named after a cargo ship that was shipwrecked here in 1983. The ship's remains are now a popular photo op, and the beach itself is a stunning sight, with its white sand and turquoise waters.

To get to Navagio Beach, you can take a boat tour from Zakynthos Town or Agios Nikolaos. There are also a few hiking trails that lead to the beach, but these are quite challenging.

3.2.2 Porto Limnionas

Porto Limnionas is a secluded beach located in the north of Zakynthos. The beach is surrounded by cliffs and lush vegetation, and the water is a crystal-clear turquoise. Porto Limnionas is a great place to relax and swim, and it's also a popular spot for snorkeling and diving.

To get to Porto Limnionas, you can take a boat tour from Zakynthos Town or Agios Nikolaos. There is also a hiking trail that leads to the beach, but this is quite challenging.

3.2.3 Gerakas Beach

Gerakas Beach is a protected area that is home to a large colony of loggerhead sea turtles. The beach is located in the south of Zakynthos, and it's one of the most important nesting beaches for sea turtles in the Mediterranean.

Gerakas Beach is a great place to go if you want to see sea turtles in their natural habitat. The beach is also a popular spot for swimming, sunbathing, and hiking.

To get to Gerakas Beach, you can take a bus from Zakynthos Town or Agios Nikolaos. The beach is accessible by a hiking trail as well.

3.2.4 Marathonisi (Turtle Island)

Marathonisi, also known as Turtle Island, is a small island located off the coast of Zakynthos. The island is a popular spot for swimming, sunbathing, and hiking. It's also a great place to go if you want to see sea turtles.

To get to Marathonisi, you can take a boat tour from Zakynthos Town or Agios Nikolaos. There is also a walking trail that leads to the island.

I hope this gives you a good overview of some of the best beaches and coastal areas in Zakynthos. If you're planning a trip to the island, be sure to add these beaches to your list!

3.3 Zakynthos National Marine Park

The Zakynthos National Marine Park is a protected area that encompasses the southern part of the island of Zakynthos. It was established in 1999 to protect the loggerhead sea turtle (Caretta caretta), which is a critically endangered species. The park is also home to a variety of other marine life, including fish, dolphins, and seabirds.

3.3.1 Caretta-Caretta Sea Turtles

The loggerhead sea turtle is the largest sea turtle in the Mediterranean Sea. They can grow up to 6 feet long and weigh up to 1,000 pounds.

Loggerhead turtles are an important part of the marine ecosystem, and they play a vital role in the food chain. They eat jellyfish, squid, and fish, and they help to keep the populations of these animals in check.

How to get to the Caretta-Caretta Sea Turtles

The best way to see the Caretta-Caretta sea turtles is to take a boat tour in the Zakynthos National Marine Park. These tours typically depart from Kalamaki Beach or Laganas Beach. The tours will take you to the beaches where the turtles nest, and you may even be able to see them swimming in the water.

3.3.2 Blue Caves

The Blue Caves are a natural wonder located on the northern coast of Zakynthos. They are formed by limestone cliffs that have been eroded by the sea over thousands of years. The caves are filled with crystal-clear water that reflects the sunlight, creating a magical blue glow.

How to get to the Blue Caves

The best way to see the Blue Caves is to take a boat tour. These tours typically depart from Agios Nikolaos or Volimes. The tours will take you to the caves, and you will be able to swim and snorkel in the clear blue water.

Here are some additional things to know about the Zakynthos National Marine Park:

 The park is open year-round, but the best time to visit is during the summer months, when the turtles are more active.

 There are a number of rules and regulations in place to protect the turtles and the marine environment. For example, it is illegal to disturb the turtles or their nests.

There are a number of tour operators that offer boat tours in the Zakynthos National Marine Park. Be sure to choose a tour operator that is committed to protecting the environment.

3.4 Zakynthos Hiking and Nature Trails

With a range of routes to select from, ranging in difficulty from basic to difficult, Zakynthos is a hiker's paradise. You can discover a trail that's ideal for you, whether you want to take a leisurely stroll through an olive grove or a challenging climb to the summit of a mountain.

Here are three of the best hiking and nature trails in Zakynthos:

3.4.1 Mt. Skopos

Mt. Skopos is the highest mountain on Zakynthos, and it offers stunning views of the island and the surrounding sea. The hike to the top is challenging, but it's worth it for the views.

To get to Mt. Skopos, you can drive to the village of Volimes and park your car at the trailhead. The hike starts off through a forest of pine trees, and then it climbs up through the rocks and scrubland. The views from the top are amazing, and you can see all the way to the coast.

3.4.2 Keri Cliffs

The Keri Cliffs are a series of dramatic limestone cliffs that rise up from the sea. There are a number of hiking trails that lead to the cliffs, and you can also take a boat trip to see them from the water.

One of the best trails to the Keri Cliffs is the one that starts at the village of Keri. The trail follows the coast for a while, and then it climbs up to the cliffs. The views from the top are incredible, and you can see the Blue Caves in the distance.

3.4.3 Neda Waterfalls

The Neda Waterfalls are a series of cascading waterfalls that are located in the north of Zakynthos. The waterfalls are surrounded by lush vegetation, and they make for a beautiful and refreshing hike.

To get to the Neda Waterfalls, you can drive to the village of Anogia and park your car at the trailhead. The hike starts off through a forest of plane trees, and then it leads to the waterfalls.

The waterfalls are located in a gorge, and you can walk behind the falls and feel the spray on your face.

These are just a few of the many hiking and nature trails that you can find on Zakynthos. So lace up your hiking boots and explore the island's natural beauty!

How to get to each trail:

Mt. Skopos: You can drive to the village of Volimes and park your car at the trailhead.

Keri Cliffs: You can drive to the village of Keri and start your hike from there. The cliffs can also be seen from the water by taking a boat ride.

Neda Waterfalls: You can drive to the village of Anogia and park your car at the trailhead.

3.5 Traditional Villages of Zakynthos

Zakynthos is not just about beaches and seascapes. It's also home to a number of charming traditional villages, each with its own unique character. Here are three of the best:

3.5.1 Volimes

Volives is a small village perched on a hilltop, overlooking the Ionian Sea. It's a great place to get a taste of traditional Greek life, with its narrow streets, whitewashed houses, and bougainvillea-lined lanes. Volimes is also home to a number of Byzantine churches and monasteries, as well as some excellent restaurants and tavernas.

How to get there: Volimes is located in the northeastern part of Zakynthos, about 15 kilometers from the town of Zakynthos. You can use a cab, bus, or vehicle to get there.

3.5.2 Keri

Keri is another beautiful village located on the northeastern coast of Zakynthos. It's known for its stunning clifftop views, as well as its traditional architecture. Keri is also a great place to go hiking, swimming, and snorkeling.

How to get there: Keri is located about 10 kilometers from the town of Zakynthos. You can use a cab, bus, or vehicle to get there.

3.5.3 Agios Leon

Agios Leon is a small fishing village located on the southwestern coast of Zakynthos. It's a great place to relax and enjoy the laid-back Greek lifestyle. Agios Leon is also home to a number of beautiful beaches, including the secluded Navagio Beach.

How to get there: Agios Leon is located about 30 kilometers from the town of Zakynthos. You can use a cab, bus, or vehicle to get there.

Other traditional villages to visit:

Argassi: This village is located on the east coast of Zakynthos and is a popular tourist destination. It's home to a number of hotels, restaurants, and bars.

Tsilivi: This village is located on the north coast of Zakynthos and is another popular tourist destination. It's known for its long sandy beaches and its vibrant nightlife.

Laganas: This village is located on the south coast of Zakynthos and is known for its party atmosphere. It's a great place to go if you're looking for a lively night out.

3.6 Zakynthos Nightlife and Entertainment

Zakynthos is a party island, and there are plenty of opportunities to let loose and have fun after dark. Here are three of the best places to go for nightlife on Zakynthos:

3.6.1 Laganas Strip

Zakynthos's party epicenter is Laganas, and the Laganas Strip is where it all takes place. The atmosphere is vibrant and the mile-long strip of bars, clubs, and restaurants is constantly crowded with people. This is the location to be if you want a crazy night out.

How to get there: Laganas is located on the south coast of Zakynthos, and it's easily accessible by bus or taxi from anywhere on the island.

3.6.2 Tsilivi

Tsilivi is another popular party destination on Zakynthos, and it's a bit more laid-back than Laganas. The nightlife here is still lively, but it's not as hectic as in Laganas. There are plenty of bars and clubs to choose from, and the beach is just a short walk away.

How to get there: Tsilivi is located on the north coast of Zakynthos, and it's easily accessible by bus or taxi from anywhere on the island.

3.6.3 Bohali Hill

If you're looking for a more sophisticated nightlife experience, then Bohali Hill is the place for you. This hilltop area is home to some of the best restaurants and bars on Zakynthos, and the views of the town and the sea are incredible. In the summer, there are often live music events and DJ sets on Bohali Hill, and the atmosphere is always buzzing.

How to get there: Bohali Hill is located in the center of Zakynthos Town, and it's a short walk from the waterfront. You can also take the cable car up to Bohali Hill for stunning views of the town and the sea.

So there you have it, three of the best places to go for nightlife on Zakynthos. Whether you're looking for a wild night out or a more sophisticated evening, you're sure to find something to your liking on this party island.

Here are some other things to keep in mind when planning your Zakynthos nightlife:

The best time to go out is during the summer months, when the weather is warm and there are more events happening.

If you're on a budget, there are plenty of bars and clubs that offer free entry.

If you're looking for a specific type of music, do some research before you go out so you can find the right place.

Drink wisely, and stay on the safe side.

3.7 Shopping and Souvenirs

Zakynthos is a shopper's paradise, with everything from traditional Greek souvenirs to high-end designer labels. Whether you're looking for a unique piece of jewelry, a traditional hand-woven basket, or a bottle of locally-produced olive oil, you're sure to find it on Zakynthos.

3.7.1 Local Products and Crafts

If you're looking for something truly unique to take home from your trip to Zakynthos, be sure to check out the local products and crafts. Here are some of the most well-liked products:

Kilims: These colorful rugs are made from hand-woven wool and are a traditional souvenir of Zakynthos. You can find them at most markets and souvenir shops on the island.

Hand-woven baskets: These baskets are made from locally-sourced materials and are perfect for storing all your beachy treasures. You can find them at many of the small shops in the villages of Zakynthos.

Olive oil: Zakynthos is known for its high-quality olive oil, so be sure to pick up a bottle or two to take home. You can find olive oil at most supermarkets and souvenir shops on the island.

Honey: Zakynthos also produces some of the best honey in Greece. You can find honey at most markets and souvenir shops on the island.

3.7.2 Markets and Boutiques

There are several markets and boutiques on Zakynthos where you can find local products and souvenirs. Here are some of the most well-liked:

Zakynthos Market: This is the largest market on the island and is a great place to find everything from fresh produce to traditional souvenirs. The market is located in the center of Zakynthos Town and is open every day.

Argassi Market: This market is located in the popular resort town of Argassi and is a great place to find souvenirs and beachwear. Except for Sunday, the market is open every day.

Lagada Boutiques: This area of Zakynthos is known for its high-end boutiques and designer stores. You can find everything from clothes to jewelry to home decor at Lagada.

How to Get There

Most of the markets and boutiques on Zakynthos are easily accessible by foot or by public transportation. If you're staying in Zakynthos Town, you can easily walk to the Zakynthos Market or the Argassi Market. If you're staying in another area of the island, you can take a bus or taxi to the nearest market or boutique.

4. Insider Tips and Recommendations

4.1 Off-the-Beaten-Path Gems

Zakynthos is a popular tourist destination, but there are still plenty of off-the-beaten-path gems to be found. Listed here are my favorites:

Agios Nikolaos: This small fishing village on the east coast is home to a beautiful beach, a charming harbor, and a few traditional tavernas. It's the perfect place to relax and soak up the Greek atmosphere.

[How to get there: Take a bus from Zakynthos Town to Agios Nikolaos. The journey takes around 30 minutes.]

Makris Gialos: This long, sandy beach is located on the east coast, just a short distance from Agios Nikolaos. It's an excellent spot for swimming, tanning, and strolling.

[How to get there: Take a bus from Zakynthos Town to Makris Gialos. The journey takes around 45 minutes.]

Porto Limnionas: This secluded cove is located on the west coast of Zakynthos. It's surrounded by towering cliffs and has crystal-clear waters. It's a great place to go for a swim, snorkel, or simply relax on the beach.

[How to get there: You can take a boat from Zakynthos Town to Porto Limnionas. The journey takes around 1 hour.]

Skinari Lighthouse: This lighthouse is located at the northern tip of Zakynthos. It offers stunning views of the Ionian Sea and the surrounding coastline. It's a great place to go for a hike or simply enjoy the scenery.

[How to get there: You can drive to Skinari Lighthouse, or you can take a bus from Zakynthos Town. The journey takes around 1 hour.]

Cape Marathi: This cape is located on the west coast of Zakynthos. It's home to a number of caves, including the Blue Caves. It's a great place to go for a boat trip or simply explore the coastline.

[How to get there: You can take a boat from Zakynthos Town to Cape Marathi. The journey takes around 1 hour.]

These are just a few of the many off-the-beaten-path gems that can be found on Zakynthos. If you're looking for a more authentic Greek experience, be sure to check them out.

Additional tips:

 If you're looking for a truly unique experience, try visiting Zakynthos during the off-season (October-May). The island is much less crowded during this time, and you'll be able to enjoy the peace and quiet.

 If you're on a budget, there are plenty of affordable ways to explore Zakynthos. You can stay in a hostel, cook your own meals, and use public transportation.

If you're looking for something to do besides sunbathing and swimming, there are plenty of other activities to enjoy on Zakynthos. You can go hiking, biking, sailing, or windsurfing.

4.2 Hidden Beaches and Coves

Porto Limnionas Beach : This beach is located in a secluded cove and is surrounded by towering cliffs. The beach is only accessible by a short hike, which makes it a great place to go for a peaceful swim or to explore the surrounding area.

[How to get there: Drive to the village of Keri and follow the signs to the beach. The hike to the beach is about 20 minutes long.]

Madrakia Beach : This beach is located in a small cove and is surrounded by lush vegetation. The beach is only accessible by boat, which makes it a great place to go for a peaceful swim or to explore the surrounding area.

[How to get there: You can take a boat from the village of Agios Sostis or Alykes.]

Kaminia Beach : This beach is located in a secluded cove and is surrounded by rocky cliffs. The beach is only accessible by a short hike, which makes it a great place to go for a peaceful swim or to explore the surrounding area.

[How to get there: Drive to the village of Kaminia and follow the signs to the beach. The hike to the beach is about 15 minutes long.]

Secluded Beach (No Name) : This beach is located in a small cove and is surrounded by cliffs. The beach is not accessible by road, so you'll need to hike or take a boat to get there.

[How to get there: You can hike to the beach from the village of Agios Sostis. The hike is about 45 minutes long.]

These are just a few of the many hidden beaches on Zakynthos. If you're looking for a unique and special beach experience, be sure to check out one of these hidden gems.

Here are some additional tips for finding and enjoying hidden beaches on Zakynthos:

Be prepared for a bit of adventure. Getting to some of the hidden beaches on Zakynthos can be a bit challenging, but it's worth it for the peace and quiet.

Be respectful of the environment. These beaches are often secluded and unspoiled, so it's important to leave no trace behind.

Enjoy the peace and quiet. These beaches are a great place to relax and escape the hustle and bustle of everyday life.

4.3 10 Best Local Restaurants

1. Alektor

Alektor is a family-run taverna in the heart of Zakynthos Town. It's a great place to try traditional Greek dishes, like moussaka, souvlaki, and grilled octopus. The service is friendly and the prices are reasonable.

How to get there: Alektor is located on Solomos Street, just a short walk from the waterfront.

2. Spartakos Taverna

Spartakos Taverna is a seafood restaurant located in Agios Nikolaos. It's a popular spot for locals and tourists alike, and the fresh fish is always cooked to perfection. The menu also includes a variety of other Greek dishes, as well as vegetarian options.

How to get there: Spartakos Taverna is located on the main road in Agios Nikolaos.

3. Nostimon Imar

Nostimon Imar is a traditional Greek restaurant located in Laganas. It's a great place to try authentic Zakynthos cuisine, like pastitsada (a lamb and pasta dish) and bourbouraki (fried zucchini flowers). The service is excellent and the prices are very reasonable.

How to get there: Nostimon Imar is located on the main road in Laganas.

4. To Kyma

To Kyma is a seafood restaurant located in Tsilivi. It's a great place to enjoy fresh fish and stunning views of the Ionian Sea. The menu also includes a variety of other Greek dishes, as well as vegetarian options.

How to get there: To Kyma is located on the beach in Tsilivi.

5. La Sponda

La Sponda is a fine-dining restaurant located in Keri. It's a great place to celebrate a special occasion or enjoy a romantic meal. The menu features creative Greek cuisine, as well as an extensive wine list.

How to get there: La Sponda is located on the clifftop in Keri.

6. The Olive Tree

The Olive Tree is a vegetarian restaurant located in Zakynthos Town. It's a great place to try healthy and delicious vegetarian food. The menu features a variety of salads, wraps, and mains, as well as a selection of vegan and gluten-free options.

How to get there: The Olive Tree is located on Solomos Street, just a short walk from the waterfront.

7. Meltemi

Meltemi is a traditional Greek taverna located in Agios Sostis. It's a great place to try authentic Zakynthos cuisine, like moussaka, souvlaki, and grilled octopus. The service is friendly and the prices are reasonable.

How to get there: Meltemi is located on the main road in Agios Sostis.

8. Zorbas

Zorbas is a Greek restaurant located in Kalamaki. It's a great place to enjoy traditional Greek cuisine in a lively atmosphere. The menu features a variety of Greek dishes, as well as a selection of meze (small plates).

How to get there: Zorbas is located on the main road in Kalamaki.

9. Akrotiri

Akrotiri is a seafood restaurant located in Agios Ioannis. It's a great place to enjoy fresh fish and stunning views of the Ionian Sea. The menu also includes a variety of other Greek dishes, as well as vegetarian options.

How to get there: Akrotiri is located on the clifftop in Agios Ioannis.

10. The Blue Eye

The Blue Eye is a restaurant located in the village of Anafonitria. It's a great place to enjoy traditional Greek cuisine and stunning views of the Blue Eye, a natural spring that is said to have healing properties.

How to get there: The Blue Eye is located in the village of Anafonitria. You can take a taxi or bus from Zakynthos Town.

4.4 Authentic Zakynthian Experiences

If you want to experience the real Zakynthos, you need to go beyond the beaches and tourist traps. Here are a few tips for finding authentic Zakynthian experiences:

Avoid the south coast. The south coast is the most touristy part of the island, and it's also where you'll find the most crowded beaches. If you want to experience a more authentic side of Zakynthos, head to the north or west coasts.
[How to get there: You can get to the north or west coasts by bus, car, or taxi. There are also

ferries that run between the different parts of the island.]

Visit a traditional village. There are many traditional villages on Zakynthos, each with its own unique character. Some of the most popular villages include Volimes, Keri, and Agios Nikolaos.

[How to get there: You can get to the traditional villages by bus, car, or taxi. There are also ferries that run between the different parts of the island.]

Go hiking or biking. Zakynthos is a great place to go hiking or biking. There are numerous trails available, varying in difficulty. You can find trails in the mountains, along the coast, and even through olive groves.

[How to get there: You can get to the hiking and biking trails by bus, car, or taxi. There are also ferries that run between the different parts of the island.]

Visit a local winery. Zakynthos is home to several wineries, where you can sample the island's delicious wines. Some of the most popular wineries include Robola Zakynthos, Gentilini, and Zante Wineries.

[How to get there: You can get to the wineries by bus, car, or taxi. There are also ferries that run between the different parts of the island.]

Attend a traditional festival. Zakynthos hosts a number of traditional festivals throughout the year. These festivals celebrate everything from the island's history and culture to its local produce. Some of the most popular festivals include the Zakynthos Carnival, the Festival of the Olive, and the Festival of the Sea.

[How to get there: You can get to the traditional festivals by bus, car, or taxi. There are also ferries that run between the different parts of the island.]

These are just a few ideas for finding authentic Zakynthian experiences. By following these tips, you can discover a side of the island that most tourists never see.

Here are some additional tips for finding authentic Zakynthian experiences:

Talk to the locals. They're the best source of information about what to do and see on the island.

Get off the beaten track. There are many hidden gems on Zakynthos, so don't be afraid to explore.

Be open to new experiences. Zakynthos is a diverse island, so be prepared to try new things.

With a little effort, you can find authentic Zakynthian experiences that will stay with you long after your vacation is over.

4.5 Photography Spots

Zakynthos is a photographer's paradise, with its stunning beaches, crystal-clear waters, and dramatic cliffs. Here are a few of the island's best photography spots:

Cameo Island Footbridge: This iconic spot is located just off the coast of Zakynthos Town. The footbridge leads to a tiny island that's home to a chapel and a few olive trees. The views from the bridge are simply stunning, and it's a great place to capture the sunset.
Take a boat from Zakynthos Town to Cameo Island to get there. It takes roughly 15 minutes to get on the boat.]

Port Agios Sostis: This picturesque port is located on the southern coast of Zakynthos. The harbor is surrounded by whitewashed houses and a small church. The views from the port are amazing, and it's a great place to capture the sunrise or sunset.
[How to get there: Drive or take a bus to Port Agios Sostis.]

Chapel of Agios Nikolaos: This tiny chapel is perched on a cliff overlooking Navagio Beach. The chapel is only accessible by boat, and it's a popular spot for photographers. The views from the chapel are breathtaking, and it's a great place to capture the beauty of Navagio Beach.

[How to get there: Take a boat from Zakynthos Town to Navagio Beach. It takes about 45 minutes to get on the boat.

Keri "Lighthouse" restaurant: This restaurant is located on the clifftops above Keri Beach. The restaurant has a large terrace with stunning views of the beach and the surrounding cliffs. It's a great place to enjoy a meal and capture some amazing photos.

[How to get there: Drive or take a bus to Keri Beach. The restaurant is located on the clifftops above the beach.]

Ionian Sunset Cafe: This cafe is located on the cliffs above Porto Limnionas Beach. The cafe has a large terrace with stunning views of the beach and the surrounding cliffs. It's a great place to enjoy a drink and capture some amazing photos of the sunset.

[How to get there: Drive or take a bus to Porto Limnionas Beach. The cafe is located on the cliffs above the beach.]

Porto Roxa Beach: This secluded beach is located on the southern coast of Zakynthos. The beach is surrounded by red cliffs and crystal-clear waters. It's a great place to relax and capture some amazing photos of the beach and the surrounding cliffs.

[How to get there: Drive or take a bus to Porto Roxa Beach. The beach is located on a small road off the main road.]

Keri Beach: This beautiful beach is located on the southern coast of Zakynthos. Cliffs surround the beach, and the ocean is glistening. It's a great place to relax, swim, and capture some amazing photos.

[How to get there: Drive or take a bus to Keri Beach. The beach is located on the main road.]

These are just a few of the many photography spots on Zakynthos. With its stunning scenery, there's something for everyone to capture on camera. So get out there and explore!

Tips for Taking Great Photos on Zakynthos

Go early in the morning or late in the afternoon. This is when the light is the most beautiful and you'll have fewer people in your photos.

Use a tripod. This will help you keep your camera steady and prevent blurry photos.

Experiment with different angles. Don't be afraid to get creative and try different angles to capture the beauty of Zakynthos.

Be patient. Sometimes the best photos take a little bit of patience. If you don't immediately get the ideal shot, don't give up.

4.6 Cultural Etiquette and Customs

If you're planning a trip there, it's important to be aware of the local customs and etiquette. This will help you avoid any awkward situations and make the most of your visit.

Dress Code

In general, Zakynthos is a fairly casual island. However, there are a few places where you'll want to dress more formally. For example, if you're planning on visiting a church or a museum, it's best to dress modestly. You'll also want to avoid wearing beachwear in town.

Tipping

Tipping is not expected in Zakynthos, but it is appreciated. If you do decide to tip, a small amount is sufficient.

Greetings

The traditional Greek greeting is a kiss on each cheek. However, this is not always done in Zakynthos. If you're not sure what to do, it's always best to err on the side of caution and just shake hands.

Politeness

Greeks are very polite people. It's important to be polite when you're in Zakynthos. This means saying please and thank you, and holding doors open for people.

Photography

It's generally okay to take photos of people in Zakynthos. However, it's always best to ask permission first. This is especially important if you're taking photos of children.

Public Displays of Affection

Public displays of affection are not as common in Zakynthos as they are in some other countries. If you're planning on holding hands or kissing in public, it's best to be discreet.

Bargaining

Bargaining is not common in Zakynthos. However, if you're buying souvenirs or other items from street vendors, you may be able to haggle a lower price.

Getting Around

Driving is the greatest way to travel about Zakynthos. Buses and taxis are also offered, though. There's a considerable chance that a resort where you're staying will have a shuttle bus that may take you to the beach or other well-known tourist attractions.

Following these tips will help you make a good impression on the locals and have a more enjoyable trip to Zakynthos. Just remember to be polite, respectful, and dress appropriately, and you'll be sure to have a great time.

5. Itineraries for a Perfect Trip

5.1 One-Week Itinerary: Highlights of Zakynthos

This one-week itinerary will help you see the highlights of Zakynthos in a relaxed and efficient way.

Day 1: Arrive in Zakynthos Town and check into your hotel.

Day 2: Explore Zakynthos Town. Visit the Venetian Castle, the Byzantine Museum, and the Church of St. Nicolaos. Take a walk through the old town and enjoy the architecture.

Day 3: Visit Navagio Beach. This iconic beach is only accessible by boat, so you'll need to take a tour from Zakynthos Town. The beach is surrounded by cliffs and has a shipwreck on the shore, making it a truly unique sight.

Day 4: Visit the Blue Caves. These caves are located on the north coast of Zakynthos and are known for their bright blue waters. You can take a boat tour to the caves and swim inside.

Day 5: Relax on one of Zakynthos' many beaches. There are beaches to suit all tastes, from secluded coves to lively resorts.

Day 6: Visit Marathonisi Island. This small island is home to a colony of loggerhead sea turtles. You can take a boat trip to the island and see the turtles in their natural habitat.

Day 7: Depart Zakynthos.

Transportation:

Driving is the most convenient way to get around Zakynthos. You'll have the opportunity to see the island at your own speed as a result of this.

You can also get around by bus, but this can be slower and less convenient.

There are also taxis available, but they can be expensive.

Cost:

The cost of this itinerary will vary depending on your budget. However, you can expect to spend around €1,000 for a week-long trip.

This is just a suggested itinerary, so feel free to adjust it to fit your own interests and preferences. With so much to see and do on

Zakynthos, you're sure to have a memorable vacation.

5.2 Two-Week Itinerary: Exploring Every Corner

Day 1:

 Arrive in Zakynthos Town and check into your hotel.

[1 hour]

 Take a walk around the town and explore the Venetian Castle, the Byzantine Museum, and the Church of St. Nicolaos.

[3-4 hours]

 Have dinner in a traditional Greek taverna.

[2 hours]

Day 2:

Take a boat trip to Navagio Beach.

[4-5 hours]

Swim in the crystal-clear waters and explore the shipwreck.

[2-3 hours]

Have lunch on the beach.

[1 hour]

Day 3:

Visit the Blue Caves.

[3-4 hours]

Take a boat ride through the caves and marvel at the stunning blue waters.

[2-3 hours]

Go snorkeling or diving in the caves.

[1-2 hours]

Day 4:

Drive to the Keri Peninsula and visit the Keri Caves.

[2 hours]

Hike to the top of the cliffs for stunning views of the coastline.

[2 hours]

Go swimming in the clear waters below.

[1 hour]

Day 5:

Visit Marathonisi Island.

[2 hours]

See the loggerhead sea turtles that nest on the island.

[1 hour]

Go swimming in the clear waters around the island.

[1 hour]

Day 6:

Drive to the Zakynthos National Marine Park.
[2 hours]
Go hiking or biking in the park.
[3 hours]
Visit the Zakynthos Bird Observatory and see some of the island's native bird species.
[1 hour]

Day 7:

Visit the Zakynthos Olive Grove.
[2 hours]
Learn about the history of olive growing on the island.
[1 hour]

Go for a walk through the grove and enjoy the peace and quiet.

[1 hour]

Day 8:

Visit the Zakynthos Byzantine Museum.

[2 hours]

Learn about the history of Byzantine culture on the island.

[1 hour]

Visit the Zakynthos Folklore Museum.

[1 hour]

Day 9:

Relax on one of Zakynthos' many beautiful beaches.

[3-4 hours]

Go shopping in Zakynthos Town.

[2 hours]

Have dinner in a restaurant with live music.

[2 hours]

Day 10:

Depart from Zakynthos.

[1 hour]

Total Transportation Cost:

Boat trip to Navagio Beach: €50

Boat trip to the Blue Caves: €40

Car rental: €300

Bus tickets: €50

Total Cost:

Accommodation: €1,000

Food: €500

Activities: €200

Transportation: €650

Total Time:

10 days

Of course, this itinerary is merely a suggestion. It can be modified to fit your personal preferences and interests.

5.3 Family-Friendly Itinerary

5.3 Family-Friendly Itinerary

Day 1:

Arrive in Zakynthos Town and check into your hotel.
[2 hours]

Take a walk around the town and explore the Venetian Castle, the Byzantine Museum, and the Church of St. Nicholas.

[3 hours]

Have dinner at a traditional Greek restaurant in the old town.

[1 hour]

Day 2:

Take a boat trip to Navagio Beach.

[4 hours]

Swim in the crystal-clear waters and explore the shipwreck.

[2 hours]

Have lunch on the beach.

[1 hour]

Day 3:

Visit the Blue Caves.

[3 hours]

Go snorkeling or diving in the caves.

[2 hours]

Have lunch at a seaside restaurant.

[1 hour]

Day 4:

Visit the Zakynthos Turtle Centre.

[2 hours]

Learn about the loggerhead sea turtles that live on the island.

[1 hour]

Go for a swim at Gerakas Beach, a protected nesting ground for the turtles.

[2 hours]

Day 5:

 Relax at a beach or pool.

[4 hours]

 Do some souvenir shopping in Zakynthos Town.

[2 hours]

 Enjoy your last dinner in Greece.

[1 hour]

Total time: 18 hours

Cost of transportation:

Boat trip to Navagio Beach: €30 per person

Blue Caves tour: €25 per person

Zakynthos Turtle Centre: €10 per person

Gerakas Beach: €5 per person

This is just a suggested itinerary, of course. You can adjust it to fit your family's interests and preferences.

5.4 Adventure Seekers' Itinerary

Day 1:

Arrive in Zakynthos Town and check into your hotel.
[1 hour]
Rent a car and drive to Keri Beach.
[30 minutes]
Hike to the top of Keri Lighthouse for panoramic views of the island.
[1 hour]
Go snorkeling in the crystal-clear waters off Keri Beach.
[2 hours]

Have dinner in Zakynthos Town and enjoy the vibrant nightlife.

[3 hours]

Day 2:

Take a boat trip to the Blue Caves.

[4 hours]

Swim in the Blue Caves and marvel at their otherworldly beauty.

[2 hours]

Visit Navagio Beach, a shipwreck beach that is only accessible by boat.

[1 hour]

Go kayaking or stand-up paddleboarding in the Zakynthos Channel.

[2 hours]

Have dinner in Agios Nikolaos and watch the sunset over the water.

[2 hours]

Day 3:

Go canyoning in the Zakynthos Mountains.
[4 hours]

Hike through the lush vegetation and swim in the refreshing waterfalls.
[3 hours]

Visit the Zakynthos Donkey Sanctuary and learn about the work they do to protect the island's donkeys.
[1 hour]

Have dinner in Zakynthos Town and enjoy a traditional Greek feast.
[3 hours]

Total cost of transportation:

Car rental: €50/day

Boat trip to the Blue Caves: €30/person

Kayaking or stand-up paddleboarding: €20/hour

Canyoning: €50/person

Total time commitment:

3 days

14 hours of activities

This itinerary is perfect for those who love adventure and want to experience the best that Zakynthos has to offer. From hiking and snorkeling to canyoning and kayaking, there is something for everyone on this itinerary. And with the Blue Caves and Navagio Beach, you'll be treated to some of the most stunning scenery in the world.

5.5 Relaxation and Wellness Retreat

Are you looking for a way to relax and rejuvenate on your next trip to Zakynthos? If so, then a relaxation and wellness retreat is the perfect option for you. This itinerary will take you to some of the most beautiful and relaxing spots on the island, where you can enjoy everything from massages and yoga to hiking and swimming.

Day 1:

 Arrive in Zakynthos Town and check into your hotel.

[1 hour]

 Take a walk around the town and explore the Venetian architecture.

[2 hours]

 Have dinner at a traditional Greek restaurant.

[1 hour]

Day 2:

Visit the Blue Caves.

[3 hours]

Go for a swim in the crystal-clear waters.

[1 hour]

Enjoy a boat trip to Marathonisi, also known as Turtle Island.

[2 hours]

Day 3:

Visit the Zakynthos Spa and have a massage.

[2 hours]

Go for a hike in the hills above Zakynthos Town.

[3 hours]

Enjoy the sun while unwinding on the beach.

[2 hours]

Day 4:

Attend a yoga class at a neighborhood gym.

[2 hours]

Visit the Byzantine Museum of Zakynthos.

[1 hour]

Have dinner at a restaurant with a view of the sunset.

[1 hour]

Day 5:

Fly home or continue your travels.

[1 hour]

Transportation:

Driving is the most convenient way to get around Zakynthos. You'll have the opportunity to see the island at your own speed as a result of this.

You can also get around by bus, but this will take longer.

The cost of transportation will vary depending on how you choose to get around.

Cost:

The cost of this itinerary will vary depending on your budget.

However, you can expect to spend around €1,000 for a 5-day trip.

This relaxation and wellness retreat is the perfect way to escape the hustle and bustle of everyday life and reconnect with yourself. You'll experience the beauty of Zakynthos, relax your body and mind, and come home feeling refreshed and rejuvenated.

Additional Tips

If you're looking for a more affordable option, you can stay in a hostel or Airbnb.

If you're on a tight schedule, you can combine some of the activities into one day.

If you're interested in learning more about the history and culture of Zakynthos, you can visit the Archaeological Museum or the Folklore Museum.

6. Practical Information

6.1 Health and Safety Tips

Stay hydrated. The weather in Zakynthos can be hot and sunny, so it's important to stay hydrated. Drink plenty of water throughout the day, especially if you're planning on being active.

Protect yourself from the sun. The sun's rays can be very strong in Zakynthos, so it's important to protect yourself from them. Apply sunscreen every two hours and wear clothing with an SPF of 30 or higher. To protect your face and eyes, you should also put on a cap and sunglasses.

Be aware of the wildlife. Zakynthos is home to a variety of wildlife, including sea turtles, dolphins, and snakes. It's important to be aware of the wildlife and to respect their habitats. Don't feed or touch the animals, and stay away from their nests.

Be careful when swimming. The waters around Zakynthos can be dangerous, especially if you're not a strong swimmer. Be careful when swimming in the ocean, and don't swim alone.

Be aware of your surroundings. Zakynthos is a safe island, but it's always a good idea to be aware of your surroundings. Don't leave your valuables unattended, and be careful when walking around at night.

Here are some additional tips to help you stay safe and healthy in Zakynthos:

Get travel insurance. Travel insurance can help you cover medical expenses, lost luggage, and other unexpected costs.

Pack first-aid supplies. This includes things like bandages, antibiotic ointment, and pain relievers.

Learn some basic Greek. This will help you communicate with the locals and get around.

Be patient. The pace of life in Zakynthos is much slower than in many other parts of the world. If things don't always go as expected, don't be shocked.

6.2 Money and Currency Exchange

The currency of Zakynthos, and all of Greece, is the euro (EUR). There are 100 cents in a euro.

How can I exchange my currency for euros?

You can exchange your currency for euros at banks, currency exchange bureaus, and some hotels. The best exchange rates are usually offered at banks, but they may have stricter opening hours. Currency exchange bureaus are often open longer hours, but they may offer slightly lower exchange rates.

Can I use my credit or debit card in Zakynthos?

Yes, you can use your credit or debit card in most shops and restaurants in Zakynthos. However, it is a good idea to have some cash on hand, as not all businesses accept cards.

What are some tips for budgeting my money in Zakynthos?

Here are a few tips for budgeting your money in Zakynthos:

Do your research. Before you go, take some time to research the average prices of things like food, drinks, and activities in Zakynthos. You can use this to create a budget and prevent overspending.

Be prepared to haggle. In some cases, you may be able to haggle for a lower price on souvenirs or other items. This is especially true in markets and street stalls.

Take advantage of free activities. There are many free activities to enjoy in Zakynthos, such as swimming in the sea, hiking, and exploring the island's villages.

Avoid tourist traps. Tourist traps are often overpriced and not worth your time or money. Do some research before you go to make sure you're not wasting your money.

I'm on a tight budget. What are some ways to save money in Zakynthos?

Here are a few ways to save money in Zakynthos:

Cook your own meals. Eating out can be expensive in Zakynthos. Making your own food is a terrific method to cut costs if you're on a tight budget.

Stay in a hostel or Airbnb. Hotels can be expensive in Zakynthos. If you're on a tight budget, staying in a hostel or Airbnb is a great way to save money.

Take advantage of free activities. As mentioned above, there are many free activities to enjoy in Zakynthos. This is a fantastic method to cut costs on your trip.

Use public transportation. Public transportation is a great way to get around Zakynthos without having to rent a car. If you're traveling on a tight budget, this can help you save a ton of money.

6.3 Communication and Internet Access

Keeping in Touch

Zakynthos is a modern island with good communication facilities. You'll be able to stay in touch with friends and family back home easily.

Phones

There are several phone companies operating on Zakynthos, including Vodafone, Cosmote, and Wind. You can buy a SIM card from any of these companies at a local shop or supermarket.

Internet Access

There are plenty of places to get online on Zakynthos. Most hotels and apartments have Wi-Fi, and there are also plenty of internet cafes around the island.

Staying Safe Online

As with anywhere, it's important to be careful when using the internet on Zakynthos. Be sure to only use secure websites, and don't give out any personal information that you don't want to share.

Here are some tips for staying safe online on Zakynthos:

Only use secure websites. Look for the https://:// at the beginning of the website address.

Don't give out any personal information that you don't want to share. This includes your name, address, phone number, or credit card information.

Be careful about what you click on. If you're not sure about a link, don't click on it.

Keep your software up to date. This includes your operating system, browser, and antivirus software.

By following these tips, you can stay safe online and enjoy your trip to Zakynthos without any worries.

Here are some other ways to stay connected on Zakynthos:

Use a messaging app like WhatsApp or Viber.

Post on social media.

Send emails.

Use a VoIP service like Skype or Google Hangouts.

No matter how you choose to stay connected, you'll be sure to stay in touch with friends and family back home while you're enjoying your vacation on Zakynthos.

6.4 Local Laws and Etiquette

Laws

Some of the most important laws to be aware of include:

Speed limits: The speed limit in built-up areas is 50 km/h and the speed limit outside built-up areas is 90 km/h.

Drinking and driving: The legal blood alcohol limit in Greece is 0.05%.

Littering: Littering is illegal in Greece and you can be fined if you are caught.

It is also important to be aware of the laws regarding the environment, as Zakynthos is a protected area. For example, it is illegal to pick wildflowers or to damage the sea turtles that nest on the island.

Etiquette

In addition to the laws, there are also some important etiquette rules to be aware of in Zakynthos. For example:

Dress code: It is generally considered polite to dress modestly in Greece. This means covering your shoulders and knees when you are in public.

Tipping: Tipping is not expected in Greece, but it is appreciated. A small tip of a few euros is usually enough.

Greetings: When you meet someone in Greece, it is customary to shake hands. You should also say "hello" and "goodbye".

Conclusion

By following these laws and etiquette rules, you can help to ensure that you have a safe and enjoyable stay in Zakynthos.

Here are some additional tips to help you stay safe and respectful in Zakynthos:

Keep an eye on your surroundings and adopt security measures to prevent small-time theft.

Respect the local culture and customs.

Learn a few basic Greek phrases.

Be responsible with your alcohol consumption.

Be respectful of the environment.

6.5 Useful Phrases in Greek

Greetings and Basic Phrases:
1. Γεια σας (Ya sas) - Hello (formal)
   Pronunciation: YAH sas

2. Γεια σου (Ya su) - Hello (informal)
   Pronunciation: YAH soo

3. Καλημέρα (Kaliméra) - Good morning
   Pronunciation: kah-lee-MEH-ra

4. Καλησπέρα (Kalispéra) - Good evening
   Pronunciation: ka-lee-SPER-a

5. Καληνύχτα (Kalinýchta) - Goodnight
   Pronunciation: ka-lee-NEEKH-ta

6. Ευχαριστώ (Efcharistó) - Thank you
   Pronunciation: ef-hah-ree-STOH

7. Παρακαλώ (Parakaló) - Please
   Pronunciation: pah-rah-kah-LOH

8. Ναι (Nai) - Yes
   Pronunciation: neh

9. Όχι (Óchi) - No
   Pronunciation: OH-hee

10. Συγνώμη (Sygnómi) - Excuse me
    Pronunciation: seen-GHO-mee

11. Γεια σας (Ya sas) - Goodbye (formal)
    Pronunciation: YAH sas
12. Γεια σου (Ya su) - Goodbye (informal)
    Pronunciation: YAH soo

Introductions and Socializing:

13. Πώς σε λένε; (Pós se léne?) - What's your name?

  Pronunciation: pohs seh LEH-neh?

14. Με λένε... (Me léne...) - My name is...

  Pronunciation: meh LEH-neh...

15. Πού είσαι; (Pou eísai?) - Where are you from?

  Pronunciation: poo EE-seh?

16. Είμαι από... (Eímai apó...) - I'm from...

  Pronunciation: EE-meh ah-POH...

17. Χαίρω πολύ (Chaíro polý) - Nice to meet you

  Pronunciation: KHEH-roh POH-lee

18. Πώς είσαι; (Pós eísai?) - How are you?

  Pronunciation: pohs EE-seh?

19. Καλά, ευχαριστώ (Kalá, efcharistó) - Fine, thank you

Pronunciation: kah-LAH, ef-hah-ree-STOH

20. Τι κάνεις; (Ti káneis?) - What are you doing?

Pronunciation: tee KAH-nees?

21. Ας πάμε για ένα ποτό (As páme gia éna potó) - Let's go for a drink

Pronunciation: as PAH-meh yah EH-nah po-TOH

22. Πού μπορώ να βρω...; (Pou boró na vro...?) - Where can I find...?

Pronunciation: poo boh-ROH nah vroh...?

23. Μπορείς να με βοηθήσεις; (Boreís na me voithíseis?) - Can you help me?

Pronunciation: boh-REES nah meh vee-THEE-sees?

24. Πού είναι η τουαλέτα; (Pou eínai i toualéta?) - Where is the bathroom?

Pronunciation: poo EEN-eh ee too-ah-LEH-ta?

25. Το αγαπημένο μου φαγητό είναι... (To agapiméno mou fagitó eínai...) - My favorite food is...

Pronunciation: toh ah-gah-pee-MEH-noh moo fah-YEE-toh EEN-eh...

Asking for Directions:

26. Πώς φτάνω στο...; (Pós ftáno sto...?) - How do I get to...?

Pronunciation: pohs FTAH-noh stoh...?

27. Δείξε μου τον δρόμο προς... (Díxe mou ton drómo pros...) - Show me the way to...

Pronunciation: THEE-kseh moo ton DROH-moh pros...

28. Πού είναι το κέντρο; (Pou eínai to kéntro?) - Where is the city center?

   Pronunciation: poo EEN-eh toh KEN-tro?

29. Πού μπορώ να πάρω το λεωφορείο; (Pou boró na páro to leoforeío?) - Where can I take the bus?

   Pronunciation: poo boh-ROH nah PAH-roh toh leh-oh-foh-REE-oh?

Shopping and Dining:

30. Πόσο κοστίζει αυτό; (Póso kostízei aftó?) - How much does this cost?

   Pronunciation: POH-soh kohs-TEE-zeh af-TOH?

31. Θα ήθελα έναν καφέ, παρακαλώ (Tha íthela énan kafé, parakaló) - I would like a coffee, please.

Pronunciation: THAH EE-THEH-la EH-nahn kah-FEH, pah-rah-kah-LOH

32. Μιλάτε αγγλικά; (Miláte angliká?) - Do you speak English?

Pronunciation: mee-LAH-teh ahn-GLEE-kah?

33. Μπορώ να πληρώσω με πιστωτική κάρτα; (Boró na pliróso me pistotikí kárta?) - Can I pay with a credit card?

Pronunciation: boh-ROH nah plee-ROH-so meh piste-tee-KEE KAHR-ta?

34. Μια τραπεζαρία για δύο, παρακαλώ (Mia trapezaría gia dýo, parakaló) - A table for two, please.

Pronunciation: mee-ah trah-peh-zah-REE-ah yah DEE-oh, pah-rah-kah-LOH

35. Έχετε συστάσεις για μέρη για φαγητό; (Échete systáseis gia méri gia fagitó?) - Do you have any recommendations for places to eat?

Pronunciation: EH-heh-te seh-stah-SEES yah MEH-ree yah fah-YEE-toh?

Emergencies:

36. Βοήθεια! (Voítheia!) - Help!

Pronunciation: voh-EE-thee-ah!

37. Έχω χάσει τον δρόμο (Écho chásei ton drómo) - I'm lost.

Pronunciation: EH-hoh KHAA-see ton DROH-moh

38. Χρειάζομαι ιατρική βοήθεια (Chreiazómai iatriki voítheia) - I need medical help.

Pronunciation: khree-AH-zoh-meh ee-at-ree-KEE voh-EE-thee-ah

39. Που είναι το νοσοκομείο; (Pou eínai to nosokomeío?) - Where is the hospital?

Pronunciation: poo EE-nay toh noh-soh-koh-MEE-oh?

149

40. Καλέστε την αστυνομία (Kaléste tin astynomía) - Call the police.

Pronunciation: kah-LEH-ste teen ah-stee-noh-MEE-ah

41. Χάσαμε τις αποσκευές μας (Chásame tis aposkevés mas) - We've lost our luggage.

Pronunciation: KHAH-sah-meh tees ah-poh-ske-VEHS mas

Feelings and Expressions:

42. Είμαι χαρούμενος (Eímai charoúmenos) - I am happy.

Pronunciation: EE-meh kha-roo-MEH-nos

43. Λυπάμαι (Lypámai) - I am sorry.

Pronunciation: lee-PAH-meh

44. Πώς νιώθεις; (Pós nióṯheis?) - How do you feel?

Pronunciation: pohs nee-OH-theis?

45. Είμαι κουρασμένος (Eịmai kourasménos) - I am tired.

Pronunciation: EE-meh koo-rah-SMEH-nos

46. Πονάει εδώ (Ponáei edó) - It hurts here.

Pronunciation: poh-NAH-ee eh-DOH

47. Είμαι πεινασμένος (Eịmai peinasménos) - I am hungry.

Pronunciation: EE-meh pee-nahs-MEH-nos

48. Είμαι δίψαση (Eịmai dípsasi) - I am thirsty.

Pronunciation: EE-meh DEEP-sah-see

49. Πώς λέγεται αυτό; (Pós légetai aftó?) - What is this called?

Pronunciation: pohs LEH-geh-teh af-TOH?

50. Πού μπορώ να βρω ένα φαρμακείο; (Pou boró na vro éna farmakeío?) - Where can I find a pharmacy?

Pronunciation: poo boh-ROH nah vroh EH-nah fahr-mah-KEE-oh?

Transportation:

51. Πού είναι ο σταθμός του μετρό; (Pou eínai o stathmós tou metró?) - Where is the subway station?

Pronunciation: poo EE-neh o stah-THMOS too meh-TROH?

52. Πότε φεύγει το τρένο; (Póte feúgei to tréno?) - When does the train leave?

Pronunciation: POH-teh FEV-yei to TRE-no?

53. Πόσο κοστίζει ένα εισιτήριο; (Póso kostízei éna eisitírio?) - How much is a ticket?

Pronunciation: POH-soh kohs-TEE-zeh EH-na
ee-see-TEE-ree-oh?

54. Πού είναι η στάση λεωφορείων; (Pou eínai i
stási leoforeíon?) - Where is the bus stop?

Pronunciation: poo EE-nai ee STAH-see
leh-oh-foh-REE-on?

55. Ποιος είναι ο κοντινότερος αεροδρόμιο;
(Poios eínai o kontinóteros aerodrómio?) - What
is the nearest airport?

Pronunciation: pee-OS EE-nai o
kon-tee-NOH-teh-ros eh-ro-DRO-mee-oh?

At the Beach:
56. Πού είναι η παραλία; (Pou eínai i paralía?) -
Where is the beach?

Pronunciation: poo EE-nai ee pah-RA-lee-ah?

57. Θα πάω για μια βουτιά (Tha páo gia mia
voutiá) - I will go for a swim.

Pronunciation: thah PAH-o yah mee-AH voo-TYAH

58. Μπορείτε να μου δανείσετε μια πετσέτα; (Boreíte na mou daneísete mia petséta?) - Can you lend me a towel?

Pronunciation: boh-REY-te na moo tha-NEY-se-te MEE-a pe-TSE-ta?

59. Χρειάζομαι ηλιογραφία (Chreiazómai iliografía) - I need sunscreen.

Pronunciation: khree-AH-zo-meh ee-lee-o-gra-FEE-a

60. Πού μπορώ να νοικιάσω ξαπλώστρες; (Pou boró na noikiáso xaplóstres?) - Where can I rent sunbeds?

Pronunciation: poo boh-ROH nah noy-KEE-aso ksa-PLO-stres?

61. Πού μπορώ να αγοράσω αναπνευστήρα; (Pou boró na agoráso anapneystíra?) - Where can I buy a snorkel?

Pronunciation: poo boh-ROH nah a-gho-RA-so a-na-pnev-stee-RA?

62. Έχετε ομπρέλες προς ενοικίαση; (Échete ompréles pros enoikíasi?) - Do you have umbrellas for rent?

Pronunciation: E-hete om-PRAY-les pros en-oy-KEE-as-ee?

In the Hotel:

63. Έχω κράτηση (Écho krátisi) - I have a reservation.

Pronunciation: EH-hoh KRAH-tee-see

64. Θα ήθελα να κάνω check-in (Tha íthela na káno check-in) - I would like to check-in.

Pronunciation: THAH EE-THEH-la nah KA-no chek-in

65. Πού είναι η υποδοχή; (Pou eínai i̱ ypodochí̱?) - Where is the reception?

Pronunciation: poo EE-nai ee ee-poh-DOH-chee

66. Θέλω ένα δίκλινο δωμάτιο (Thélo̱ éna díklino do̱mátio) - I want a double room.

Pronunciation: THE-loh EH-na DEEK-lee-no doh-MAH-tee-oh

67. Πού είναι το ασανσέρ; (Pou eínai to asansér?) - Where is the elevator?

Pronunciation: poo EE-nai toh ah-sahn-SER?

68. Ποιες είναι οι ώρες του πρωινού γεύματος; (Poies eínai oi óres tou pro̱inou gévmatos?) - What are the breakfast hours?

Pronunciation: pee-EHS EE-nai ee OH-res too pro-EE-noo GEF-ma-tos?

69. Μπορώ να έχω περισσότερες πετσέτες; (Boró na écho perissóteres petsétes?) - Can I have more towels?

Pronunciation: boh-ROH nah EH-ho peh-ris-SO-te-res pe-TSE-tes?

70. Πού μπορώ να βρω το Wi-Fi password; (Pou boró na vro to Wi-Fi password?) - Where can I find the Wi-Fi password?

Pronunciation: poo boh-ROH nah vroh toh Wi-Fi password?

6.6 Emergency Contacts

Avoiding Emergencies

Be aware of your surroundings. This is especially important at night, when crime rates are higher.

Don't carry valuables with you. If you must bring them, keep them hidden.

Be cautious when talking to strangers. Don't give out your personal information.

If You Do Have an Emergency

Call the police. The emergency number in Greece is 112.

Go to the nearest hospital. The main hospital on Zakynthos is the General Hospital of Zakynthos, located in Zakynthos Town.

Contact your embassy or consulate. They can provide you with assistance if you need it.

Here are some additional emergency contacts:

Fire department: 199
Ambulance: 166
Coast Guard: 108
Tourist Police: 171

I hope you have a safe and enjoyable trip to Zakynthos!

7. Conclusion

7.1 Recap and Highlights

As we come to the end of our Zakynthos Travel Guide, let's take a moment to recap and highlight some of the key points we've covered. Throughout this guide, we've explored the unspoiled natural beauty of Zakynthos, delving into its pristine beaches, captivating landscapes, and unique attractions. We've provided insider tips, itineraries, and recommendations to help you make the most of your trip to this remarkable island.

From the breathtaking Shipwreck Beach (Navagio) to the enchanting Blue Caves, Zakynthos offers a plethora of experiences that will leave you in awe. We've also dived into the local culture and traditions, giving you a deeper understanding of the island's rich heritage.

7.2 Final Thoughts

Zakynthos truly is a hidden gem waiting to be discovered. Its untouched landscapes, crystal-clear waters, and warm hospitality make it an ideal destination for every type of traveler. Whether you seek relaxation, adventure, or a blend of both, Zakynthos has something to offer.

As you embark on your journey to this unspoiled natural paradise, we encourage you to embrace the spirit of exploration and immerse yourself in the beauty that surrounds you. Take the time to connect with the locals, savor the delicious cuisine, and create unforgettable memories.

We hope that this ultimate guide has provided you with the knowledge and inspiration to plan your perfect trip to Zakynthos. May your adventure be filled with wonder, joy, and a deep appreciation for the wonders of nature.

Safe travels and enjoy your unforgettable experience on the unspoiled island of Zakynthos!

Made in United States
Troutdale, OR
07/26/2023

11570278R00096